- view

dandelafe

- *view*

daniel delafe

Phoenix Pyre Publishing
2018

First published by Phoenix Pyre Publishing

First Edition: August, 2018
Printed in the United States of America

Cover design by the author.
Image on front and back cover from *La grāt danse macabre
des homes*, printed in Lyon by Mathias Huss, 1499.
Image on title page:
In ictu oculi by Juan de Valdés Leal, c. 1671.
Photograph of the author taken by Miles Hendrickson.

ISBN-10: 0692161791
ISBN-13: 978-0692161791

To those who understand that some of these poems are more serious than others, which is quite deliberate, and that this book is directed at no one in particular, but a zeitgeist. These are merely the musings of a Fool.

contents

"...take a strict view of their excrements, and, from the colour, the odour, the taste, the consistence, the crudeness or maturity of digestion, form a judgment of their thoughts and designs; because men are never so serious, thoughtful, and intent, as when they are at stool..."

—Jonathan Swift, from *Gulliver's Travels*

- view

so far
my poems
haven't been
short or simple
enough for
mass appeal
in this day
and age

- *tldr*

another view
    rushes into the eyes
        assiduously crafted

- the point of this

words can be a gourmet meal
of intricacy and complex flavors
with layers and layers of meaning
or words can be served up quick
like fast food for a culture of
automatons that loathe having to
figure anything out for themselves
that loathe anything too complicated
so let me spoon-feed you the meaning
let me hand it to you on a silver platter
do you like the taste? is there enough salt?

- fast food wordplay for social media

every individual is a sacred
methuselah
with roots in our ancestors'
graves
and branches reaching up like
hands
as a hieroglyphic sign for our
spirits

- *ka*

scent you leave
behind on my pillow
is the scent of jasmine
scent of your presence
which fills my heart
like a chalice
until it's overflowing
like an overused metaphor
why write about
anything else
but you?

- romantic relationships are the most important
subject

i will now compare you
to some inanimate object
or some flower
some season
some constellation
the sun the moon and the stars
to express your infinite
beauty and how you
get better with age
like wine or cellared tobacco
(no one wants to hear
the latter though)
or how each time i look at you
i fall deeper and deeper
into an illusion
i project onto you

- *you are like a so and so*

fight for
    my identity
fight for
    my group
why change
    myself first
when I
    can change
the world?

- tolstoy says we're doing it backwards

here's a deep aphorism
for you
which i
have broken up
into pieces
so i could call it poetry

- *from the bottom of the sea with cemented feet*

death is not prejudiced
and does not discriminate
he loves to dance
with everyone equally

- *social justice reaper*

never display
anything but the positive
we want to be envied
only show the best
a finger touching
the top of the Eiffel Tower
or the stunning view
we witnessed tonight

more through our phones than with our eyes

- *this picture needs no filter*

i just wish
every time a heart
was broken
someone else expressed
exactly how they felt
in simple language
so i could share it
on my wall
so my ex-lover
will hopefully see it
so i can receive
the validation i
so desperately desire
with encouraging
hearts and comments

- it's almost like he wrote this for me

in the motion of
my mother's wheelchair wheels
and the dirt on
my father's planting hands
the pen in
my grandmother's wrinkling fingers
and the worries in
my brother's troubled mind

- where you'll find me

love is what we write about
when we don't know
what else to write about
but what we call love is not love
if we only write about ourselves
and some other person
we are infatuated with
or have been hurt by
and ignore everything else
happening around us

- love encompasses more than one object of affection

sturdy and time-tested
like vellum
that life's movable type
has pressed
with language and rhythm
and bound
in red morocco with a
gilt spine
strong enough to hold
these pages

- *endurance*

would it comfort you
if i told you love was just a feeling?
that even if you've lost it
it will fly back to you
if you hold onto hope?
well, it's not

a feeling is simply
one facet of it.

love is…

- *the words i write to comfort you*

…an action.
and before all else,
love is knowledge
of yourself and another.
and it takes work
to gain knowledge,
but it's easier to
just believe
love is merely
a feeling.

you can always
take the easy way
and write a poem
about feelings

- *actions speak louder than terrible poetry (i would
know because i write terrible poetry)*

i do not write this
to make you feel
better about yourself.
there's enough
of that trite
going around.
maybe you're
really doing
something wrong.
find out.
observe yourself.

- to make you feel empowered

solipsistic sentences flow from
the glowing luminescent rectangles
of circuitry and liquid-crystal displays.

- *myopia*

you are worthy of all the love
he never gave you
so now i'm telling you
(in a sentence
i simply broke up
to look more poetic)
that he made a big mistake
when he left you,
because you're great,
you're special.

is that what you want to hear?
it might be, yet perhaps that's not
what you *need* to hear.
maybe you don't really
know yourself—not yet.

*- love isn't saying what someone wants to hear but
what someone needs to hear*

much of what we produce
is like excrement.
it comes out for a reason
but should be flushed
or buried afterward
rather than consumed
or put on exhibition.
i don't always follow
my own advice though.

- pantagruelism

set a skull
upon this book
upon your desk.
stare at it and remember:
evanescent are the trappings.

- memento mori

some say "artists" are self-centered creatures.
many certainly are.
don't become the "artist" who only writes
about yourself—
your feelings,
your thoughts,
your experiences.
that's easy to do.
how much of that is really even *you?*
look outside of "i"
see yourself in others, others in you, too,
then write about that.
become cosmic, all-encompassing—
not merely something that's trending right now.

*- it's trendy to be self-centered; become the Centre
of Centers*

it's all about
how popular
we seem
the numbers
on the screen
that is true love

- i'll follow you but then unfollow you if you don't follow me back or i'll follow you so you follow me back so i can unfollow you and hope you don't notice

must not think
too hard.
the modern poet
speaks for
a generation of
very short
attention spans.

- poetry on life support

must not feel
too deeply
or expansively
cosmic.
the modern poet
speaks for
a generation of
narcissists.

- *poetry looking at its own reflection*

this poem was
composed to fit nicely
into a square on
your smartphone screen
to be read quickly
and digested easily

- words from(for) the heart(s)

fog sits on the Hudson today.
the thunderstorms keep popping up—
booming overhead—
booming in my head.

*- family in crisis (when it rains it really does pour—
time to step up)*

scribble some
platitudes and clichés
about heartbreak
and love
and beauty
and pain.
post it.
hashtag it.
thousands of hearts.
best seller list.
voice of a generation.
am i famous yet?

- scribble

sweet-sour stench of love's silhouette
remains behind after Your presence,
a rotten apple covered in Drosophila
that will be discarded as compost;
bubbles bursting remind me of
what's truly important—
that our youth will wither;
presidents will perish;
fame will fade

- *vanitas*

i, too, see you down in catacombs of despair.
if you're holding these words in your hands
that means you are very much not alone.
sometimes simplicity in language is solace,
just knowing someone else is present,
has been through something similar,
understands you.
i get it.

- i see the appeal

so here i am
partly rebelling,
partly conforming,
hoping you can still
consume and appreciate
milk and honey as much as
Paterson and *Leaves of Grass*.

- an appeal

allow yourself to
make some errors,
even if some are people
or bad poetry.
just make sure
you learn when to say
"enough of that shit"—
because mosquitoes breed
in stagnant water.
become a flowing stream
that bloodsuckers
can't lay eggs in.

- knowledge is what protects

I like being right,
but I also like being wrong,
because the more wrong I am now
the more right I'll be later.
So in that sense,

being wrong is far more important.

*- mark grillo recommended this one appear on my
tombstone*

lift up your suffering.
raise it up high
like a trophy scar.
stop being a victim.
use this platitude to
remind you to try
before the clock melts.

- *assistance of memory*

1. myself
2. humanity (past, present, and future)
3. the page
4. the smartphone screen
5. the stage (i rarely do readings)

- who/what i write for in order of importance

a dance of death
in the information age.
all at your fingertips,
from Gutenberg's breath
pressed into the page
to data on digital lips.

- at what cost?

the plot of our stories
took an unexpected turn
the day we met each other
in Central Park in front of
the spinning merry-go-round
and sat in Sheep Meadow

- my love gets one for the sake of conforming

let me

break   it   down

for you:

love and
knowledge
are One Thing

- *dispelling common misconceptions*

I appreciate what you do
even if I don't always care for it.
But I gotta keep
the conversation alive,
because we are all neurons
within this Great Mind,
and I hope these little squiggles
make you *think*
rather than simply feel.
They are a synapse
sending out electric charges
for you to view in cyberspace—
to learn, to grow, to heal.

- for the modern poets of the screen

an equality of letters
is a novel concept
but i like to elevate
some things above others

to hide Treasures in shape,
in the subtleties of capitals,
presence or absence of periods,
words of intended obscurity
I expect you to look up—
significances that must be
dug up and brushed off,
making you perform
mental archaeology.

- *legerdemain*

as a poet I intend to become Proteus—

fluid and old

Some things are best expressed in complex figures
of strung-together ideas and symbols set in motion
by a flowing Hand that does not rest and keeps
hiding more and more and more nuances and
meanings for you to uncover in miniscule little
details within what is intentionally revealed on the
surface of a run-on sentence before the fingers ever
leave the keyboard or the pen ever lifts from the
page, gathered like dug-up bones moved to a
charnel house or placed in an ossuary.

and other things—
well, Polonius said it best in *Hamlet*, I suppose.

- *brevity at length*

ABOUT THE AUTHOR

Daniel DeLafe was born and raised in Elizabeth, New Jersey, where he still resides. In 2014 he received his B.A. in English & Writing from Kean University. He is an independent bookseller, a book collector, and an avid reader with an epic curiosity, fascinated by everything from history, comparative religion, mythology, psychology, the paranormal, esotericism and the occult, to science, world literature, poetry, and art. He occasionally enjoys drawing and painting, is a self-taught drummer/percussionist, and is partial to the company of cats, although he loves dogs as well. This is his third book of poetry.

"...and we [the Lilliputians] *conjecture it* [Gulliver's pocket watch] *is either some unknown animal, or the god that he worships; but we are more inclined to the latter opinion, because he assured us, (if we understood him right, for he expressed himself very imperfectly) that he seldom did any thing without consulting it. He called it his oracle, and said, it pointed out the time for every action of his life."*

—Jonathan Swift, from *Gulliver's Travels**

---

*I imagine the Lilliputians would think the same today, but of Gulliver's smartphone rather than his pocket watch.

www.ingramcontent.com/pod-product-compliance
Lightning Source LLC
Chambersburg PA
CBHW071933020426
42331CB00010B/2855